HERSHEY'S® RECIPES

Cinnamon Chips Gems

1 cup (2 sticks) butter or margarine, softened
2 packages (3 ounces each) cream cheese, softened
2 cups all-purpose flour
½ cup sugar
⅓ cup ground toasted almonds
2 eggs
1 can (14 ounces) sweetened condensed milk
1 teaspoon vanilla extract
1⅓ cups HERSHEY'S Cinnamon Chips, divided

1. Beat butter and cream cheese in large bowl until well blended; stir in flour, sugar and almonds. Cover; refrigerate about 1 hour.

2. Divide dough into 4 equal parts. Shape each part into 12 smooth balls. Place each ball in small muffin cup (1¾ inches in diameter); press evenly on bottom and up side of each cup.

3. Heat oven to 375°F. Beat eggs in small bowl. Add sweetened condensed milk and vanilla; mix well. Place 7 cinnamon chips in bottom of each cookie shell; fill a generous ¾ full with sweetened condensed milk mixture.

4. Bake 18 to 20 minutes or until tops are puffed and just beginning to turn golden brown. Cool 3 minutes. Sprinkle about 15 chips on top of each cookie. Cool completely in pan on wire rack. Remove from pan using small metal spatula or sharp knife. Store tightly covered at room temperature.

Makes 4 dozen cookies

Reese's® Double Peanut Butter and Milk Chocolate Chip Cookies

½ cup (1 stick) butter or margarine, softened
¾ cup sugar
⅓ cup REESE'S® Creamy or Crunchy Peanut Butter
1 egg
½ teaspoon vanilla extract
1¼ cups all-purpose flour
½ teaspoon baking soda
¼ teaspoon salt
1¾ cups (11-ounce package) REESE'S® Peanut Butter and
    Milk Chocolate Chips

1. Heat oven to 350°F.

2. Beat butter, sugar and peanut butter in medium bowl until creamy. Add egg and vanilla; beat well. Stir together flour, baking soda and salt; add to butter mixture, blending well. Stir in chips. Drop by rounded teaspoons onto ungreased cookie sheets.

3. Bake 12 to 14 minutes or until light golden brown around the edges. Cool 1 minute on cookie sheet. Remove to wire rack; cool completely.

Makes about 3 dozen cookies

Design Your Own Chocolate Cookie

1 cup (2 sticks) butter, softened
1 cup granulated sugar
¾ cup packed light brown sugar
2 teaspoons vanilla extract
½ teaspoon salt
2 eggs
2 cups all-purpose flour
½ cup HERSHEY'S Cocoa
1 teaspoon baking soda

1. Heat oven to 375°F.

2. Beat butter, granulated sugar, brown sugar, vanilla and salt in large bowl until creamy. Add eggs; beat well.

3. Stir together flour, cocoa and baking soda; gradually add to butter mixture, beating until well blended. Drop by rounded teaspoons onto ungreased cookie sheet.

4. Bake 8 to 10 minutes or until set. Cool slightly; remove from cookie sheet to wire rack. Cool completely.   *Makes about 5 dozen cookies*

Chocolate Chocolate Chip Cookies: Add 2 cups (one 12- or 11.5-ounce package) HERSHEY'S Semi-Sweet MINI CHIPS™, SPECIAL DARK® or Milk Chocolate Chips to basic chocolate batter.

Mini Kisses® Chocolate Cookies: Add 1¾ cups (10-ounce package) HERSHEY'S MINI KISSES® Milk or Semi-Sweet Chocolates to basic chocolate batter.

Mint Chocolate Chip Cookies: Add 1⅔ cups (10-ounce package) HERSHEY'S Mint Chocolate Chips to basic chocolate batter.

Chocolate Cookies with White Chips: Add 1⅔ cups (10-ounce package) HERSHEY'S Premier White Chips to basic chocolate batter.

Holiday Bits Chocolate Cookies: Add 1⅓ cups (10-ounce package) HERSHEY'S Semi-Sweet Holiday Bits to basic chocolate batter.

Chocolate Cookies with Peanut Butter Chips: Add 1⅔ cups (one 10- or 11-ounce package) REESE'S® Peanut Butter Chips or REESE'S® Peanut Butter and Milk Chocolate Chips to basic chocolate batter.

White Chip Apricot Oatmeal Cookies

¾ cup (1½ sticks) butter or margarine, softened
½ cup granulated sugar
½ cup packed light brown sugar
1 egg
1 cup all-purpose flour
1 teaspoon baking soda
2½ cups rolled oats
1⅔ cups (10-ounce package) HERSHEY'S Premier White Chips
¾ cup chopped dried apricots

1. Heat oven to 375°F.

2. Beat butter, granulated sugar and brown sugar in large bowl until fluffy. Add egg; beat well. Add flour and baking soda; beat until well blended. Stir in oats, white chips and apricots. Loosely form rounded teaspoonfuls dough into balls; place on ungreased cookie sheet.

3. Bake 7 to 9 minutes or just until lightly browned; do not overbake. Cool slightly; remove from cookie sheet to wire rack. Cool completely.

Makes about 3½ dozen cookies

Chocolate Almond Macaroon Bars

2 cups chocolate wafer cookie crumbs
6 tablespoons butter or margarine, melted
6 tablespoons powdered sugar
1 can (14 ounces) sweetened condensed milk
3¾ cups (10-ounce package) MOUNDS™ Sweetened Coconut Flakes
1 cup sliced almonds, toasted* (optional)
1 cup HERSHEY'S Semi-Sweet Chocolate Chips
¼ cup whipping cream
½ cup HERSHEY'S Premier White Chips

*To toast almonds: Heat oven to 350°F. Spread almonds evenly on shallow baking sheet. Bake 5 to 8 minutes or until lightly browned.

1. Heat oven to 350°F. Grease 13×9×2-inch baking pan.

2. Combine crumbs, melted butter and sugar in large bowl. Firmly press crumb mixture on bottom of prepared pan. Stir together sweetened condensed milk, coconut and almonds in large bowl, mixing well. Carefully drop mixture by spoonfuls over crust; spread evenly.

3. Bake 20 to 25 minutes or until coconut edges just begin to brown. Cool.

4. Place chocolate chips and whipping cream in medium microwave-safe bowl. Microwave at HIGH (100%) 1 minute; stir. If necessary, microwave at HIGH an additional 10 seconds at a time, stirring after each heating, until chips are melted and mixture is smooth when stirred. Cool until slightly thickened; spread over cooled bars. Sprinkle top with white chips. Cover; refrigerate several hours or until thoroughly chilled. Cut into bars. Refrigerate leftovers. *Makes about 36 bars*

Reese's® Peanut Butter and Milk Chocolate Chip Brownies

¾ cup HERSHEY'S® Cocoa
½ teaspoon baking soda
⅔ cup butter or margarine, melted and divided
½ cup boiling water
2 cups sugar
2 eggs
1⅓ cups all-purpose flour
1 teaspoon vanilla extract
¼ teaspoon salt
1¾ cups (11-ounce package) REESE'S® Peanut Butter and
   Milk Chocolate Chips

1. Heat oven to 350°F. Grease 13×9×2-inch baking pan.

2. Stir together cocoa and baking soda in large bowl; stir in ⅓ cup butter. Add boiling water; stir until mixture thickens. Stir in sugar, eggs and remaining ⅓ cup butter; stir until smooth. Add flour, vanilla and salt; blend completely. Stir in chips. Pour into prepared pan.

3. Bake 35 to 40 minutes or until brownies begin to pull away from sides of pan. Cool completely in pan on wire rack. Cut into squares.

Makes about 36 brownies

Layered Cookie Bars

¾ cup (1½ sticks) butter or margarine
1¾ cups vanilla wafer crumbs
6 tablespoons HERSHEY'S Cocoa
¼ cup sugar
1 can (14 ounces) sweetened condensed milk
1 cup HERSHEY'S Semi-Sweet Chocolate Chips
¾ cup SKOR® English Toffee Bits
1 cup chopped walnuts

1. Heat oven to 350°F. Melt butter in 13×9×2-inch baking pan in oven. Combine crumbs, cocoa and sugar; sprinkle over butter. Pour sweetened condensed milk evenly on top of crumbs. Top with chocolate chips and toffee bits, then nuts; press down firmly.

2. Bake 25 to 30 minutes or until lightly browned. Cool completely in pan on wire rack. Chill, if desired. Cut into bars. Store covered at room temperature. *Makes about 36 bars*

Rocky Road Brownies

1¼ cups miniature marshmallows
1 cup HERSHEY'S Semi-Sweet Chocolate Chips
½ cup chopped nuts
½ cup (1 stick) butter or margarine
1 cup sugar
2 eggs
1 teaspoon vanilla extract
½ cup all-purpose flour
⅓ cup HERSHEY'S Cocoa
½ teaspoon baking powder
½ teaspoon salt

1. Heat oven to 350°F. Grease 9-inch square baking pan. Stir together marshmallows, chocolate chips and nuts. Place butter in microwave-safe bowl. Microwave at HIGH (100% power) 1 to 1½ minutes or until melted. Add sugar, eggs and vanilla; beat with spoon until well blended. Add flour, cocoa, baking powder and salt; blend well. Spread batter in prepared pan.

2. Bake 22 minutes. Sprinkle chip mixture over top. Bake 5 minutes or until marshmallows have softened and puffed slightly. Cool completely. With wet knife, cut into squares. *Makes about 20 brownies*

Monogrammed Mini Chocolate Cakes

½ cup (1 stick) butter or margarine
3 tablespoons HERSHEY'S Cocoa
1 cup all-purpose flour
1 cup sugar
½ teaspoon baking soda
¼ teaspoon salt
⅓ cup dairy sour cream
1 egg
   Cocoa Glaze (recipe follows)
   Decorating icing in tube, desired color

1. Heat oven to 350°F. Line bottom of 13×9×2-inch baking pan with parchment or waxed paper.

2. Combine butter, ½ cup water and cocoa in small saucepan. Cook over medium heat, stirring constantly, until mixture boils; remove from heat. Stir together flour, sugar, baking soda and salt in medium bowl. Stir in hot cocoa mixture. Add sour cream and egg; beat on medium speed of mixer until well blended. Pour batter into prepared pan.

3. Bake 20 to 22 minutes or until wooden pick inserted in center comes out clean. Cool 10 minutes. Remove from pan to wire rack; carefully remove parchment paper. Cool completely.

4. Cut cake into small pieces, each about 2×1¾ inches. (Cake will be easier to cut if frozen for several hours or up to several days.) Place on wire cooling rack. Prepare Cocoa Glaze; spoon over top of each piece of cake, allowing glaze to run down sides. Allow glaze to set. Garnish with monogram, using decorating icing. Place in foil cup, if desired.

Makes about 24 mini cakes

Cocoa Glaze: Bring ½ cup water and ¼ cup (½ stick) butter to boil in small saucepan. Stir in ½ cup HERSHEY'S Cocoa. Remove from heat; cool slightly. Gradually add 3 cups powdered sugar, stirring with whisk until smooth. Stir in 2 teaspoons vanilla extract. Makes about 1½ cups glaze.

Creamy Cinnamon Chips Cheesecake

1½ cups graham cracker crumbs
1 cup plus 2 tablespoons sugar, divided
5 tablespoons butter, melted
2 packages (8 ounces each) cream cheese softened
1 teaspoon vanilla extract
3 cartons (8 ounces each) dairy sour cream
3 eggs, slightly beaten
1⅔ cups (10-ounce package) HERSHEY'S Cinnamon Chips, divided
1 teaspoon shortening (do not use butter, margarine, spread or oil)

1. Heat oven to 325°F. Combine graham cracker crumbs, 2 tablespoons sugar and melted butter in medium bowl. Press crumb mixture evenly onto bottom and about 1½ inches up side of 9-inch springform pan. Bake 8 minutes. Remove from oven.

2. Increase oven temperature to 350°F. Beat cream cheese, remaining 1 cup sugar and vanilla on medium speed of mixer until well blended. Add sour cream; beat on low speed until blended. Add eggs; beat on low speed just until blended. Do not overbeat.

3. Pour half of filling into prepared crust. Sprinkle 1⅓ cups chips evenly over filling in pan. Carefully spoon remaining filling over chips. Place in shallow baking pan.

4. Bake about 1 hour or until center is almost set. Remove from oven; cool 10 minutes on wire rack. Using knife or narrow metal spatula, loosen cheesecake from side of pan. Cool on wire rack 30 minutes more. Remove side of pan; cool 1 hour.

5. Combine shortening and remaining ⅓ cup chips in small microwave-safe bowl. Microwave at HIGH (100%) 30 seconds; stir until chips are melted. Drizzle over cheesecake; cover and refrigerate at least 4 hours. Cover and refrigerate leftover cheesecake.   *Makes 12 to 14 servings*

Dandy Cake

1 cup water
1 cup (2 sticks) butter or margarine
⅓ cup HERSHEY'S Cocoa
2 cups all-purpose flour
2 cups sugar
1 teaspoon baking soda
½ teaspoon salt
3 eggs
¾ cup dairy sour cream
¾ cup REESE'S® Creamy Peanut Butter
  Chocolate Topping (recipe follows)

1. Heat oven to 350°F. Grease and flour 15½×10½×1-inch jelly-roll pan.

2. Combine water, butter and cocoa in small saucepan. Cook over medium heat, stirring occasionally, until mixture boils; boil and stir 1 minute. Remove from heat; set aside.

3. Stir together flour, sugar, baking soda and salt in large bowl. Add eggs and sour cream; beat until well blended. Add cocoa mixture; beat just until blended (batter will be thin). Pour into prepared pan.

4. Bake 25 to 30 minutes or until wooden pick inserted in center comes out clean. Do not remove cake from pan. Spread peanut butter over warm cake. Cool completely in pan on wire rack. Prepare Chocolate Topping; carefully spread over top, covering peanut butter. Allow topping to set; cut into squares. *Makes 20 to 24 servings*

Chocolate Topping: Place 2 cups (12-ounce package) HERSHEY'S Semi-Sweet Chocolate Chips and 2 tablespoons shortening (do not use butter, margarine, spread or oil) in small microwave-safe bowl. Microwave at HIGH (100%) 1½ minutes; stir. If necessary, microwave at HIGH an additional 15 seconds at a time, stirring after each heating, just until chips are melted when stirred.

Double Peanut Clusters

1⅔ cups (10-ounce package) REESE'S® Peanut Butter Chips
 1 tablespoon shortening (do not use butter, margarine, spread or oil)
 2 cups salted peanuts

1. Line cookie sheet with waxed paper.

2. Place peanut butter chips and shortening in large microwave-safe bowl. Microwave at HIGH (100%) 1½ minutes; stir until chips are melted and mixture is smooth. If necessary, microwave an additional 30 seconds until chips are melted when stirred. Stir in peanuts.

3. Drop by rounded teaspoons onto prepared cookie sheet. (Mixture may also be dropped into small paper candy cups.) Cool until set. Store in cool, dry place.   *Makes about 2½ dozen clusters*

Butterscotch Nut Clusters: Follow above directions, substituting 1⅔ cups (10-ounce package) HERSHEY'S Butterscotch Chips for Peanut Butter Chips.

Easy Chocolate Cheese Pie

2 bars (1 ounce each) HERSHEY'S Unsweetened Baking Chocolate, broken into pieces
 ¼ cup (½ stick) butter or margarine, softened
 ¾ cup sugar
 1 package (3 ounces) cream cheese, softened
 1 teaspoon milk
 2 cups frozen whipped topping, thawed
 1 packaged crumb crust (6 ounces)
 Additional whipped topping (optional)

1. Place chocolate in small microwave-safe bowl. Microwave at HIGH (100%) 1 to 1½ minutes or until chocolate is melted and smooth when stirred.

2. Beat butter, sugar, cream cheese and milk in medium bowl until well blended and smooth; fold in melted chocolate.

3. Fold in 2 cups whipped topping; spoon into crust. Cover; refrigerate until firm, about 3 hours. Garnish with additional whipped topping, if desired.
Makes 6 to 8 servings

Chocolate Raspberry Dessert

    1 cup all-purpose flour
    1 cup sugar
    ½ cup (1 stick) butter or margarine, softened
    ¼ teaspoon baking powder
    4 eggs
    1½ cups (16-ounce can) HERSHEY'S Syrup
      Raspberry Cream Center (recipe follows)
      Chocolate Glaze (recipe follows)

1. Heat oven to 350°F. Grease 13×9×2-inch baking pan.

2. Combine flour, sugar, butter, baking powder and eggs in large bowl; beat until smooth. Add syrup; blend thoroughly. Pour batter into prepared pan.

3. Bake 25 to 30 minutes or until wooden pick inserted in center comes out clean. Cool completely in pan on wire rack. Spread Raspberry Cream Center on cake. Cover; refrigerate. Pour Chocolate Glaze over chilled dessert. Cover; refrigerate at least 1 hour before serving. Cover; refrigerate leftover dessert.

Makes about 12 servings

Raspberry Cream Center: Combine 2 cups powdered sugar, ½ cup (1 stick) softened butter or margarine and 2 tablespoons raspberry-flavored liqueur* in small bowl; beat until smooth. (A few drops red food coloring may be added, if desired.) *¼ cup raspberry preserves and 1 teaspoon water may be substituted for the raspberry-flavored liqueur.*

Chocolate Glaze: Melt 6 tablespoons butter or margarine and 1 cup HERSHEY'S Semi-Sweet Chocolate Chips in small saucepan over very low heat. Remove from heat; stir until smooth. Cool slightly.

Double Raspberry Chocolate Dessert: Substitute 1 cup HERSHEY'S Raspberry Chips for Semi-Sweet Chocolate Chips in the Chocolate Glaze.

Peanut Butter and Chocolate Mousse Pie

1 (9-inch) pie crust, baked and cooled
1⅔ cups (10-ounce package) REESE'S® Peanut Butter Chips, divided
1 package (3 ounces) cream cheese, softened
¼ cup powdered sugar
⅓ cup plus 2 tablespoons milk, divided
1 teaspoon unflavored gelatin
1 tablespoon cold water
2 tablespoons boiling water
½ cup sugar
⅓ cup HERSHEY'S Cocoa
1 cup (½ pint) cold whipping cream
1 teaspoon vanilla extract

1. Melt 1½ cups peanut butter chips. Beat cream cheese, powdered sugar and ⅓ cup milk in medium bowl until smooth. Add melted chips; beat well. Beat in remaining 2 tablespoons milk. Spread into cooled crust.

2. Sprinkle gelatin over cold water in small bowl; let stand 1 minute to soften. Add boiling water; stir until gelatin is completely dissolved. Cool slightly. Combine sugar and cocoa in medium bowl; add whipping cream and vanilla. Beat on medium speed of mixer until stiff; pour in gelatin mixture, beating until well blended. Spoon into crust over peanut butter layer. Refrigerate several hours. Garnish with remaining chips. Cover; refrigerate leftover pie. *Makes 6 to 8 servings*

Toffee Bread Pudding with Cinnamon Toffee Sauce

3 cups milk
4 eggs
¾ cup sugar
¾ teaspoon ground cinnamon
¾ teaspoon vanilla extract
½ teaspoon salt
6 to 6½ cups ½-inch cubes French, Italian or sourdough bread
1 cup SKOR® English Toffee Bits or HEATH® BITS 'O BRICKLE®
   Almond Toffee Bits, divided
   Cinnamon Toffee Sauce (recipe follows)
   Sweetened whipped cream or ice cream (optional)

1. Heat oven to 350°F. Butter 13×9×2-inch baking pan.

2. Mix together milk, eggs, sugar, cinnamon, vanilla and salt in large bowl with wire whisk. Stir in bread cubes, coating completely. Allow to stand 10 minutes. Stir in ½ cup toffee bits. Pour into prepared pan. Sprinkle remaining ½ cup toffee bits over surface.

3. Bake 40 to 45 minutes or until surface is set. Cool 30 minutes.

4. Meanwhile, prepare Cinnamon Toffee Sauce. Cut pudding into squares; top with sauce and sweetened whipped cream or ice cream, if desired.

Makes 12 servings

Cinnamon Toffee Sauce: Combine ¾ cup SKOR® English Toffee Bits or HEATH® BITS 'O BRICKLE® Almond Toffee Bits, ⅓ cup whipping cream and ⅛ teaspoon ground cinnamon in medium saucepan. Cook over low heat, stirring constantly, until toffee melts and mixture is well blended. (As toffee melts, small bits of almond will remain.) Makes about ⅔ cup sauce.

Note: This dessert is best eaten the same day it is prepared.